TOTTERING-BY-GENTLY®
ANNUAL

ANNIE TEMPEST

F

FRANCES LINCOLN LIMITED

PUBLISHERS

Frances Lincoln Limited
4 Torriano Mews
Torriano Avenue
London NW5 2RZ
www.franceslincoln.com

Tottering-by-Gently Annual
Copyright © Frances Lincoln 2010
Text copyright © Annie Tempest 2010
Illustrations copyright © Annie Tempest 2010

Mix and Match Food and Wine quiz and Wine
multiple choice quiz © Berry Bros. & Rudd 2010
Crossword puzzle © Anne Bradford 2002, 2010
Leadergram puzzle © Anne Bradford 2010

Illustrations archived and compiled
by Raymond O'Shea
Designed by Becky Clarke
Edited by Anna Sanderson

ISBN 978-0-7112-3086-6

Printed in China
Bound for North Pimmshire

9 8 7 6 5 4 3 2 1

Annie Tempest and the publisher would like to thank the
following for their contribution:
Simon Berry of Berry Bros. & Rudd (Mix and Match Food and
Wine quiz and Wine multiple choice quiz, pages 36–39);
Anne Bradford (Crossword puzzle, pages 70–71, Tottering
Word Chain, page 88, Leadergram puzzle, pages 42–44);
Julian Fellowes (Introduction, page 5) and Jeremy Musson
('History of Tottering Hall' article, pages 6–8).

Other Tottering-by-Gently books by Annie Tempest:
Out and About with the Totterings
The Totterings' Desk Diary
The Totterings' Pocket Diary
Drinks with the Totterings
Available from Frances Lincoln at www.franceslincoln.com

At Home with the Totterings
Tottering-by-Gently Vol III
Available from The Tottering Drawing Room, along with a full range of
Tottering-by-Gently licensed product, at The O'Shea Gallery, No. 4 St James's Street,
London SW1A 1EF (Telephone +44 (0)207 930 5880) or www.tottering.com

TOTTERING-BY-GENTLY ®
ANNIE TEMPEST

Annie Tempest is one of the top cartoonists working in the UK. This was recognized in 2009 with the Cartoon Art Trust awarding her the prestigious Pont Prize for the portrayal of the British Character. Annie's cartoon career began in 1985 with the success of her first book, *How Green Are Your Wellies?* This led to a regular cartoon, 'Westenders' in the *Daily Express*. Soon after, she joined the *Daily Mail* with 'The Yuppies' cartoon strip which ran for more than seven years and for which, in 1989, she was awarded 'Strip Cartoonist of the Year'. Since 1993 Annie Tempest has been charting the life of Daffy and Dicky Tottering in Tottering-by-Gently – the phenomenally successful weekly strip cartoon in *Country Life*.

Daffy Tottering is a woman of a certain age who has been taken into the hearts of people all over the world. She reflects the problems facing women in their everyday life and is completely at one with herself, while reflecting on the intergenerational tensions and the differing perspectives of men and women, as well as dieting, ageing, gardening, fashion, food, field sports, convention and much more.

Daffy and her husband Dicky live in the fading grandeur of Tottering Hall, their stately home in the fictional county of North Pimmshire, with their extended family: son and heir Hon Jon, daughter Serena, and grandchildren Freddy and Daisy. The daily, Mrs Shagpile, and love of Dicky's life, Slobber, his black Labrador, and the latest addition to the family, Scribble, Daisy's working Cocker Spaniel, also make regular appearances.

Annie Tempest was born in Zambia in 1959. She has a huge international following and has had eighteen one-woman shows, from Mexico to Mayfair. Her work is now syndicated from New York to Dubai and she has had numerous collections of her cartoons published.

2009 © Garlinda Birkbeck

THE O'SHEA GALLERY

Raymond O'Shea of The O'Shea Gallery was originally one of London's leading antiquarian print and map dealers. Historically, antiquarian galleries sponsored and promoted contemporary artists who they felt complemented their recognized areas of specialization. It was in this tradition that O'Shea first contacted *Country Life* magazine to see if Annie Tempest would like to be represented and sponsored by his gallery. In 1995 Raymond was appointed agent for Annie Tempest's originals and publisher of her books. Raymond is responsible for creating an archive of all of Annie's cartoons.

In 2003, the antiquarian side of his business was put on hold and the St. James's Street premises were finally converted to The Tottering Drawing Room at The O'Shea Gallery. It is now the flagship of a worldwide operation that syndicates and licenses illustrated books, prints, stationery, champagne, jigsaws, greetings cards, ties and much more. It has even launched its own fashion range of tweeds and shooting accessories under the label Gently Ltd.

The Tottering Drawing Room at The O'Shea Gallery is a wonderful location which is now available for corporate events of 45–125 people and is regularly used for private dinner parties catering for up to 14 people. Adjacent to St. James's Palace, the gallery lies between two famous 18th century shops: Berry Bros. & Rudd, the wine merchants and Locks, the hatters. Accessed through French doors at the rear of the gallery lies Pickering Place – not only the smallest public square in Great Britain, with original gas lighting, but it was also where the last duel in England was fought. A plaque on the wall, erected by the Anglo-Texan Society, indicates that from 1842–45 a building here was occupied by the Legation from the Republic of Texas to the Court of St. James.

Raymond O'Shea and Annie Tempest are delighted to be able to extend Tottering fans a warm welcome in the heart of historic St. James's where all the original Tottering watercolours can be seen along side a full product and print range.

To see the full range of product visit: **www.tottering.com**

MEET THE TOTTERINGS

Lord Tottering
'Dicky'

Lady Tottering
'Daffy'

Serena

Freddy

Daisy

Hon Jon

Gladys Shagpile

Scribble

Slobber

INTRODUCTION

There is nothing I love more than a jolly good annual at Christmas, and I look forward to putting my feet up with this one, containing, as it does, something for more or less everyone. Some readers may be surprised at the dazzling collection of what Daffy would call receipts, since we must all know by now that food is low, and shedding pounds is high, on her list of priorities. I suspect they are included as a kindness to Dicky. At Tottering Hall, much of the cooking falls to Mrs Shagpile and it is fairly obvious to even a casual visitor that she needs what Nanny would call 'firm guidance'. When I was last in North Pimmshire, we were given a Shagpile chicken pie and, to be honest, I wanted to call the police.

I would like to think Freddy and Daisy would enjoy the puzzles and games, if they would only close their computers and put down their mobiles for one minute, but anyway I will. And the crossword should provide fun for someone in every age group. Except possibly for Dicky, who can become a little too emotionally involved. I remember one *Times* challenge which insisted on a spelling that differed from Dicky's older, preferred version. The end came when he crumpled the paper and thrust it into the relevant page of the ancient dictionary with the cry, 'See for your bloody self!'

I grew up with annuals of all the cartoon and comic characters of the day. My favourite was a *Babar* annual and I was photographed at the tender age of about two in a pale, smocked dress, carefully stroking the charming images. Apparently about four minutes after the picture was taken, I fell into a great rage and tore it to bits with my teeth. Happy Days.

So here's wishing health and happiness to Daffy, Dicky, Serena and all, not forgetting Slobber and Scribble. And also, dear reader, to you.

Julian Fellowes

TOTTERING HERALD

MONDAY, 12TH MAY   ONE ENGLISH POUND

TOTTERING HALL PIMMSHIRE

The Seat of Viscount Tottering

Tottering Herald takes an exclusive look at the extraordinary family house of the Totterings

Tottering Hall is one of the ancient seats of North Pimmshire, and it has long been a name that evokes grandeur and longevity. Many admirers of Jane Austen will have realised that it provided the model for her novel *Damenblast Park*, in which it was the seat of the illustrious Earl of Invective.

The house was originally adapted from a 12th-century monastery, endowed by Ranulf de Titterung, sword-bearer to the Count Odeur de Brie. At the Reformation, the de Tytterings were granted the house and lands of the Abbey of St. Cistern, by a king grateful for their support against the Anabaptists. However, the de Tytterings so delighted in the ancient religious house that they became firm defenders of the old religion, as they remain today.

In 1734 the family seat, little more than the decayed rump of the monastery, was transformed into a palace in the grand Palladian manner by the elegant, if notorious, Henry 'Parsnip' Tottering – later the 1st Viscount (Fig 4). After returning from the Grand Tour of Italy he determined to build himself a house of the new fashion. There are bills and payments made to a master mason, Courage Mortar. Lord Tottering, however, let it be known that he had been the architect himself and after 1734 Courage Mortar was employed to survey Lord Tottering's plantations in Barabados and never returned to England.

Many of the fine interiors of the house date from the time of the 3rd Viscount, described by Goethe, while at the spa in Baden-Bagel: 'This tiny man is judged by his fellows a good judge of things; he has the Borghese Potato'. He married

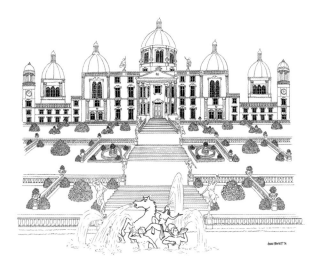

Fig 1 A drawing of the late-19th-century Italianate additions to the house by the architect Charles Cott-Blankett, including terraces planted with rhubarbs from all the countries in the world. The house was described in *The Builder* for 1899 as 'deranged'.

Fig 2 Tottering Hall today after being rejected by the National Trust as 'a nightmare of extravagant building', the house was remodelled to resemble its 18th-century appearance by Bill Trowser, a pupil of Lutyens.

Fig 3 The newly-engaged Lord Tottering and the Hon Daphne Fitzstonic-Gordons share an interest in country pursuits, 1956.

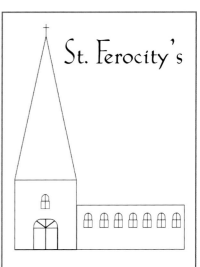

St. Ferocity's

SUMMER FETE

JULY 20TH

Gymkhana
Tombola
Archery
Morris Dancing
Comic Dog Show
WI Cake Stall
Comic Husband Show
Sheep Racing
Unicycle Riding
Pin the Tail on the Llama

PLEASE COME AND SUPPORT US

St. Ferocity's
Tottering-by-Gently
North Pimmshire

---

the extremely tall Princess Odelwigge. Cardinal Scipio Maserati referred to them in his Roman journals: 'The Principessa Tottering is like a great cathedral, milordi Tottering like a little priest in her shadow'.

The 6th Viscount 'Spotted Dick' Tottering (Fig 5) married, in 1894, Dysunity Blister, and shortly after became a passionate big game hunter spending much of his time abroad. The Blisters had the monopoly on exporting custard to India, and Lady Tottering poured a fortune into the house. Liking, she told her architect, Charles Cott-Blankett, the 'Italianified air of the house', she resolved to rebuild the house with an

extraordinary neo-Baroque vivacity, adding two wings with several domes of beaten copper and an elaborate Italianate terraced garden (Fig 1).

By the 1930s the custard bubble had burst and the glory of Tottering had become a huge burden. Jonquil Thimbleton-Finds, adviser to the National Trust, visited the house in 1942. Mr Thimbleton-Finds wrote that it was 'a hideous business: the young Lord Tottering, a friend of my brother Tarquin at Eton, collected me from Rottingbeam station in a car borrowed from his groom; the house is a nightmare of extravagant building of the 1890s, all domed up with nowhere to go but with many good 18th- and early-19th-century interiors and portraits. We ate lunch in a gloomy dining room, used in the afternoons by refugee children for table tennis. The wine was very good'.

The National Trust turned down the house, and Lord Tottering considered selling it to a prep school. However, he took heart when the Ministry of Works removed the domes 'for the safety of the refugee school children'. The west wing was pulled down after a fire in 1952 and the house modelled to its present form (Fig 2) by Bill Trowser, a pupil of Lutyens. In 1957 Lord Tottering married the Hon Daphne Fitzstonic-Gordons, of another of the ancient Pimmshire county families

(Fig 3). During the 1960s and 1970s the young and energetic Lady Tottering breathed new life into the house: reorganising the furnishings, selling and burning judiciously and removing the garden terraces.

The success of her work is surely to be judged by the remark made by Diana Tailfeather, the interior designer, who wrote in 1980: 'This most delightful of houses taught me a great deal about English country-house taste. Their secret is so obvious and so simple: they do nothing for centuries, but do it very well'.

Fig 4 The plans for the 18th-century house are seen in the portrait of the 'Parsnip', the 1st Viscount Tottering. An enthusiastic Grand Tourist and well-known wrestler, he claimed to be the designer of the house.

Fig 5 'Spotted Dick' Tottering, the 6th Viscount, who married the custard heiress Dysunity Blister, was a world-class big-game hunter. His trophies decorate most of the east wing, including the smoking room where they surround his portrait by Oscar Egg, RA.

EARN EXTRA

£££££££

TEACHING ESSENTIAL LIFE SKILLS

AIR KISSING

WHICH KNIFE?

WHICH CHAMPAGNE?

SHOOTING ON TARGET

HOUSEKEEPER TRAINING

STATELY DECOR

DINING FOR DOGS

CALL 873425 NOW!

Oh, that's my Great Uncle Cecil - totally eccentric, you know...

He used to read the 'Tottering Herald' at the top of his voice to the sheep in the park...

A sort of early 'Have I Got News For Ewe...

1995©ANNIE TEMPEST.

I take pride in dusting your ancestors - I know all their names, you know...

ANNIE TEMPEST ©1999

This one's Sir J. Reynolds...

I suppose he was a cross-dresser like our Eric, was he, madam?..

One of my wifes friends talked the hind legs off that one...

9

DICKY AND DAFFY'S NIGHT OUT

"Are you nearly ready? Or is that just the undercoat?"

The 'who's driving tonight' discussion...

Just look at the amount of make-up that child's wearing - she can't be more than 14 years old....

We've just got to accept that our world has been turned upside down ...

...and I suppose these days it's normal for 'lamb' to dress up as 'mutton'...

It's my husbands turn to drive so I'm drinking for two...

"I believe the red ribbon means she kicks..."

You've had about five glasses of Bollinger already, Daffy!....

I know, darling - but it doesn't seem to have gone to my head at all ...

No - it's gone to your legs...

His girls are all pretty wild, aren't they, Dicky...

Yes - I often wonder if the number of daughters a man's allocated in this life is in proportion to how bad he was in a previous life...

..and that woman on my right! All this introspective twaddle and monologues about the universe...

Oh! dear! You poor thing.. Fancy a little something before turning in?

Yes...a nice simple prep school joke would go down a treat...

Nothing nicer after a good party than kicking off your shoes...

having a quiet night cap...

... and letting your stomach muscles out...

DRESS YOUR OWN REAL WOMAN

Cut out and colour in your own Daffy, Lady Tottering doll and dress her in one of four fabulous outfits: bathing wear for the summer hols, everyday wear for an English country lady, eveningwear for a dinner party at the Parsley-Fidgetts, or pyjamas with slippers and much-needed 'hotty' for bed ….

INSTRUCTIONS

Photocopy the Daffy doll and her outfits. You can colour them in either before or after cutting them out. It may be easier before.

Cut out the paper doll and the two semi-circular base supports below. Carefully cut along the lines on the base of the doll and at the top of the base supports to create slots; taking care to cut to the full length of the marked lines.

Tip: If you feel Daffy needs some backbone to stand up straight (as befits her station), before you cut out your photocopy glue it on to a piece of lightweight card. Then cut round the doll and the card at the same time. Remember to cut out between her legs if you want her boots to fit. Do the same for the two base supports.

If you want Daffy to wear shoes, using a sharp knife, carefully cut slots where marked either side of her feet. Make sure you have plenty of padding such as newspaper or thick card underneath so you don't damage the surface you are working on.

Insert each semi-circular base support, at right angles, through the two slots in the base of the doll. They need to go the full length so that both the supports and the main edge of the base are aligned across the bottom. You can adjust this if necessary by just extending any of the slots, otherwise Daffy will fall over (and that's before she's had a glass of champagne!).

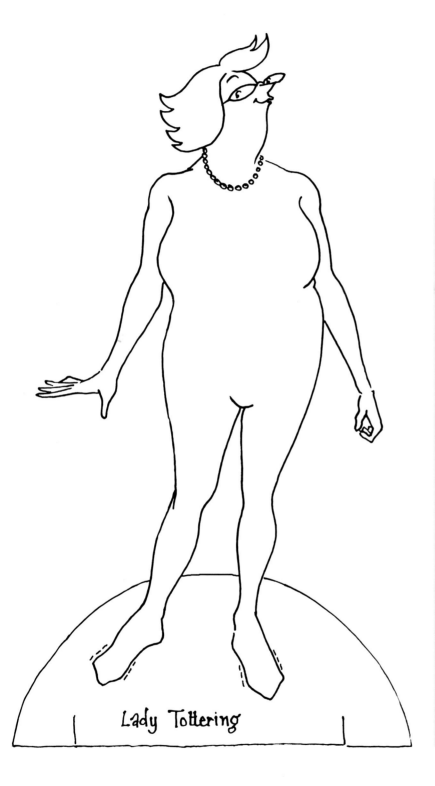

Lady Tottering

Colour in the outfits -- you can do this
before or after cutting out!

Bend the tabs to fit clothing
and accessories around the
paper doll

Daffy would not wear any patterns or
colour that would frighten the horses

It doesn't matter how I dress in town because nobody knows who I am...

It doesn't matter how I dress in the country because everyone knows who I am...

THE ENGLISH WOMAN IN THE TOWN

THE ENGLISH WOMAN IN THE COUNTRY

DRESSING FOR DINNER AT
THE PARSLEY-FIDGETTS...

Essential support
underwear for smart
evenings only

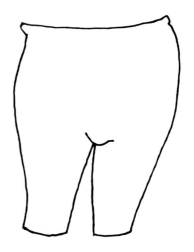

AND SO TO BED . . .

18

SAVE OUR ORGAN! SAVE OUR SOULS!

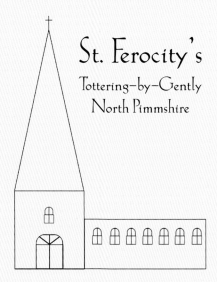

St. Ferocity's
Tottering-by-Gently
North Pimmshire

PARISH NEWSLETTER

CHURCH ANNOUNCEMENTS

- Ladies. Don't forget the jumble sale in aid of the woodworm in the organ. It's a last chance to get rid of those things not worth keeping around the house. Don't forget your husbands.
- On Thursday evenings throughout the month, Mrs Dawster-Manuel will be doing auditions for the choir. They need all the help they can get.
- Potluck supper will be on Sunday at 5.00pm. Prayer and medication to follow.
- Sunday 15th at 7.00pm there will be a hymn sing in the gardens of Tottering Hall across from the church. Bring a blanket and come prepared to sin.
- Weight Watchers will meet at 6.30pm on Mondays. Please use the large double doors at the side entrance.
- The sermon at the morning service will be 'Jesus Walks on Water'. The sermon at the evening service will be 'Searching for Jesus'.

The Lost Chapter in Genesis

So God asked him, 'What is wrong with you?' Adam said he didn't have anyone to talk to. God said that he was going to make Adam a companion and that it would be a woman. He said, 'This person will gather food for you, cook for you, and when you discover clothing, she will wash it for you. She will always agree with every decision you make. She will bear your children and never ask you to get up in the middle of the night to take care of them. She will not nag you and will always be the first to admit she was wrong when you have had a disagreement. She will never have a headache and will freely give you love and passion whenever you need it.'
Adam asked God, 'What will a woman like this cost?' God replied, 'An arm and a leg.'
Then Adam asked, 'What can I get for a rib?'
The rest, as they say, is history.

SUMMER FETE

Thank you to everyone who sent in pictures of this year's May Day Fête – held in the grounds of Tottering Hall by kind permission of Lord and Lady Tottering – a few are shown here. We are delighted to have raised the princely sum of £3355.15p for the organ fund and a jolly good time was had by all. We will reprise on July 20th!

Daisy Takes a First …

She's a Jolly Good Fellow! Lady Tottering raised £98.02p for her sponsored blindfolded unicycle ride … she lasted three seconds …

Morris and Dicky cut a dash

A capital turn out for the Comic Husband and Dog Show …

Q How would it have been different if it had been three wise women, instead of the three wise men, who visited Bethlehem over 2,000 years ago?

A The three wise women would have:
1) asked for directions
2) arrived on time
3) brought some nappies.

21

COMMON ANNUAL WEEDS...

Annual Nettle

Shepherd's Purse

Common Chickweed

Hairy Bittercress

Groundsel

Annual Meadow Grass

Hit...or

START

THE MOSQUITO FROM MZUZU

To all brunettes whom love has conned,
This comfort I repeat-oh;
If gentlemen prefer a blonde-
Then so does a mosquito...

(From Kit and The Widow's 'African Alphabet')

(Solution on page 95)

END

Missed!

A mosquito visits the bedroom at midnight...
THE FEMALE APPROACH...

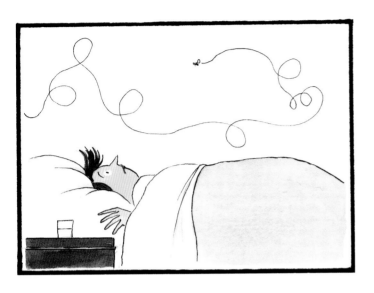

A mosquito visits the bedroom at midnight...
THE MALE APPROACH...

THE SHOOTING PARTY

gun
cartridge
butt
retriever
gamekeeper
beater
grouse
partridge
pheasant

shoot
drive
muzzle
license
shotgun
line of sight
discharge
trigger

breech
barrel
stock
stops
game
shooting party
lunch
tweeds

stalking
the guns
bag
gorse
GloriousTwelfth
purdeys
landrover
fire
brace

```
                    A D L
                  P Z W Q X S E Z Y
                Z I V E E L T T H D F N E
            M F H O L B G I T H E O E S R O G
          E G S Z C P E D C N O G L T R A F Y J
        D U H Z C O R A I E A W S I S G T T L X J
        N G T G H E E T R N S B L F S W U R U H P
      U H N F N P K W E T S A S J G D F Z N B C S O
      U T V L E Q G E R R E E Z S R E V O R D N A L
    G H V E E F G H D Q A L H S B R A C E E R U Z E A
    H D H K W I B Z B K P S P J W V J E E T N L Q V L
    F Y E Y T R A P G N I T O O H S C K S X H I P S M
  D W M T Z S E R S D E E W T Y C H F D T Q S V L H D S
  N A U W X U V R B N N V E T A X T X L A P E S U O R G
  G R M Q U O E E N O U C L R U M U H H L O Z F A O Z D
  E E U H I I L A W N G T D W H T P M K V N U C T H
  X B W Y R R L K L E R E R B L T F R I R R O W K R
  H C O F O T B A G I G L H T Q M N R N N X H C F S
  E P B L E Q E D D X R S T B Q I Z G P N F K P
  J T L G R V G Y O T Y A S A D R I V E S E C W
  O R Z S E F Z M E X E H A V B D Q Y L F V
  M M I C P V T D X K F M C T Q Q U Z C T U
  Q G G B O R Q J D V K A S E M Z I E U
  K Y G U T P I Q V C G G I U G L K
  P E X S L V L O E U M D H
  R R B U T T S K J
  D X S
```

(answers on page 95)

What do you mean, it's time I thought about giving up shooting?...

Put it this way: It's not the beaters any more who say "Nice to see you again this year, Sir..."

...It's the pheasants...

ANNIE TEMPEST © 1999

26

Look at that, Daffy! It's a stunning, crisp and sunny day...

come on, old girl...

...let's go out and shoot something...

Huge bag today. The guns will never be able to take this many birds...

I'll get the keeper to sell them to that restaurant in Rottingbeam...

I'm not sure that Kentucky fried pheasant will catch on....

27

THE TOTTERING COAT OF ARMS

ORIGINS AND MEANINGS

The use of a coat of arms arose in medieval times as a means of identifying individuals on the battlefield. If a knight was dressed head to toe in armour his face could not be seen – therefore the use of particular markings on his shield came to be used. This had the advantage that the shield could be seen easily in the confusion of battle thus identifying friend or foe. The coat of arms would also be embroidered on to the knight's tunic as well as used to identify his household.

A coat of arms was awarded to an individual – not to a family – although subsequent generations might only make minor adjustments.

The coat of arms of the current incumbents of Tottering Hall has the classic shield shape common of their English Norman aristocratic antecedents.

The gold background symbolizes the 'generosity and elevation of mind' (seen in Dicky's love of the cryptic crossword) and the green overlay symbolizes 'hope, joy and loyalty in love' – the first two particular characteristics of the distaff side of the family.

The diagonal 'bend' or scarf/shield suspender of the knight commander signifies defence or protection and is a relic from the arms of early de Tytterings who were firm defenders of the old religion (for more information see page 6).

The presence of the wellington boot symbol is the cause of much debate. Some historians insist it heralds the family's connection to Lord Wellington who visited Tottering Hall in the spring of 1816. This occasion was the first public report describing the 'Iron Duke's' boots, which had been specially adapted to his personal specification by Hoby of St. James's. This adaptation was to become the forerunner of the wellington boot we love today. However, anecdotal family history insists the presence of the green rubber symbols is simply an 'homage à Hunters'. This writer's personal opinion leans towards this second explanation – an opinion supported by the family's motto: *In Wellis Latexis Plodamus*, which is self-explanatory. The significance of the number six remains unacknowledged and a request for clarification was declined by Lord Tottering.

The crest was added to the coat of arms in 1957 on the occasion of the marriage of Lord Tottering and the Honourable Daphne Fitzstonic-Gordons.

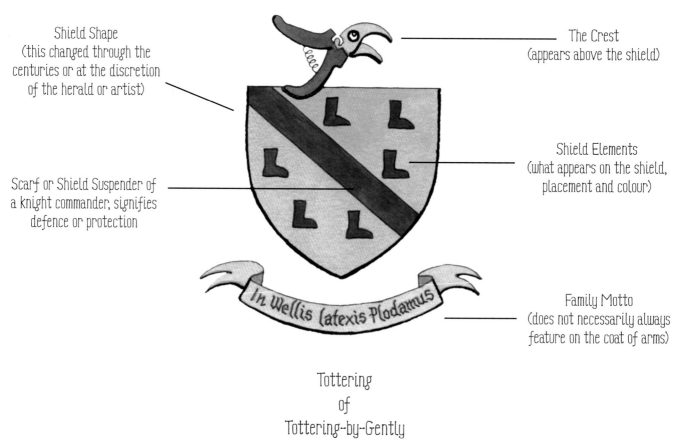

Shield Shape
(this changed through the centuries or at the discretion of the herald or artist)

The Crest
(appears above the shield)

Scarf or Shield Suspender of a knight commander, signifies defence or protection

Shield Elements
(what appears on the shield, placement and colour)

Family Motto
(does not necessarily always feature on the coat of arms)

In Wellis latexis Plodamus

Tottering
of
Tottering-by-Gently

CREATE YOUR OWN COAT OF ARMS

1 Add your family name to the bottom banner.

2 Choose or create your family's motto. Add to banner above the shield.

3 Choose your family virtues.

4 Decide if you want your shield divided in some way (diagonally or quartered).

5 Add any desired symbols to the shield. These symbols should represent something important about you and your interests.

6 Colour in as desired (see box for further information).

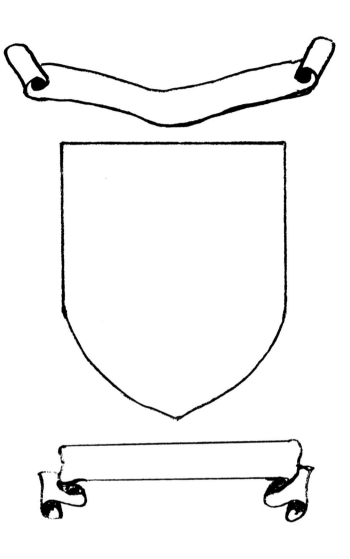

MOTTOS	VIRTUES
Drink and Be Merry	Accepting
Faithful to the End	Accomplished
Never Under Lunched	Affectionate
I Love as I Find	Ambitious
Courage and Faith	Animal Loving
In My Dog I Trust	Articulate
By Skill and Valour	Artistic
By Skill Not Force	Bravery
By Truth and Diligence	Caution
Seize the Present	Curiosity
Doughnuts before Diets	Defiance
What Will Be Will Be	Discretion
Seek and You Will Find	Forgiveness
Steady and Faithful	Focus
Heart and Hand	Generosity
Drink More Drink	Gentleness
All Courage, No Fear	Humour
Your Promises Kept	Justice
Strength Gives Glory	Loyalty
The Wounds of Life	Obedience
To God and Country	Patience
I Drink I Hope	Reliability
God is Our Strength	Sensitivity
I Will Again Hope	Sobriety
Faith Over Fortune	Steadfastness
Faith Fears Not	Strength
She Who Must be Obeyed	Trust
Live Strong	
Brave and Faithful	
Strong is the Truth	

COLOURS AND THEIR MEANINGS

Choose your colour with care as every part of the coat of arms conveys meaning.

Colour	Meaning
Gold	Generosity and elevation of the mind
Silver or White	Peace and sincerity
Red	Warrior or martyr
Blue	Truth and loyalty
Green	Hope, joy and loyalty in love
Black	Constancy or grief
Purple	Royal Majesty, sovereignty, justice
Orange	Worthy ambition
Maroon	Patient in battle and yet victorious

THE PERKS OF BEING OVER 50

1. No one expects you to run -- anywhere.
2. People no longer view you as a hypochondriac.
3. There is nothing left to learn the hard way.
4. Things you buy now won't wear out.
5. You can eat dinner at 4.00pm.
6. You can live without sex (but not without glasses).
7. You enjoy hearing about other people's operations.
8. When you have a party the neighbours don't even notice.
9. You no longer think of speed limits as a challenge.
10. You've stopped trying to hold your stomach in — no matter who walks into the room.
11. You sing along with lift music.
12. Your eyes won't get much worse.
13. Your investment in health insurance is finally beginning to pay off.
14. Your joints are more accurate meteorologists than weather forecasters.
15. In a hostage situation you are likely to be released first.

EXCLUSIVE OFFER

FEELING FAT? FED UP OF DIETING?
WOULD YOU LIKE TO HAVE YOUR CAKE AND EAT IT?

HAVE YOUR CAKE AND EAT IT ™

METRIC-FREE MEASUREMENTS
MAKE ALL THE DIFFERENCE

SAVE INCHES IN SECONDS
WITH OUR ONE-OF-A-KIND EXCLUSIVE HAVE YOUR CAKE AND EAT IT™ SLIMMING KIT
(Patent pending)

NO PILLS! NO FRILLS!
INSTANT SUCCESS GUARANTEED

It is as easy as one, two, three . . .

❶ Using your EXCLUSIVE laboratory-tested, animal-product-free Have Your Cake And Eat It™ Solution, blank out the numbers on the exclusive Have Your Cake And Eat It™ Tape Measure supplied.

❷ Using your FREE Have Your Cake And Eat It™ Marker Pen, mark every 2 inches as 1 inch (see below).

❸ Now use your unique Have Your Cake And Eat It™ Tape to check your waist . . . Yes, Your Eyes Are **Not** Deceiving You. Your waist will have shrunk by 50%
AMAZEMENT GUARANTEED!

Your EXCLUSIVE
Have Your Cake And Eat It™
kit includes:
1x Have Your Cake And Eat It™
Tape Measure
1x Have Your Cake And Eat It™
Solution
Includes FREE BONUS
Have Your Cake And Eat It™ Pen

[Self-assembly instructions included]

ONLY £29.99 with FREE P&P!
Goods supplied in discreet packaging

TO ORDER CALL FREEPHONE:
08455-CON-ME-NOW-111
www.have-your-cake-and-eat-it.com

AS SEEN ON TV

Limited Offer Only

RESULTS GUARANTEED BUT YOU WON'T GET YOUR MONEY BACK

A DAY IN THE LIFE OF SLOBBER

Breakfast...

Helping with the washing-up...

Sorting out the post...

Elevenses...

Assessing the weather...

Taking Dicky and Daffy out...

Meeting friends for a gossip...

Lunch...

Visiting the old dears...

32

Birdwatching...

Doing one's bit for the environment...

Making sure Dicky gets his exercise...

A good scratch...

Having friends over...

Getting into trouble...

Making up...

Relaxing...

Bedtime

DOGS ARE BETTER THAN CHILDREN BECAUSE THEY . . .

. . . eat less . . .

. . . don't ask for money all the time . . .

. . . are easier to train . . .

. . . normally come when called . . .

. . . never ask to drive the car . . .

. . . don't hang out with drug addicts . . .

. . . don't smoke or drink . . .

. . . don't want to wear your clothes . . .

. . . don't have to buy the latest fashions.

And, if they get pregnant, you can sell their children . . .

No wonder they're our best friends...

COLOUR YOUR OWN ... TOTTERING DRAWING ROOM

Use the list of colours below as inspiration to colour in your very own Tottering scene

Jean and I thought it would be rather fun to play girls against boys...

Burgundy	Granny's pearl white	Family titian
Claret	Absinthe green	Varicose vein blue
Rose	Shooting green	Bill envelope brown
Eau de gin	Royal blue	'In the' red
Pimm's pink	Huntsman Pink	Finger green
Grouse green	Cardigan bay	Threadbare taupe
Heather	Labrador fawn	Larder slate grey
Champagne white	Going grey	Aga cream
Gillow brown	Cocktail olive	Porridge beige
Salmon pink	Lobster bisque	Papal purple

TOTTERING WINE CELLARS

Would Dicky let you loose in his cellar to choose the wine for dinner?
How confident are you at matching the right wine to a particular food? When
you get it right it is a marriage made in heaven but when it is wrong …

Test your skills by matching the food in the left hand column with the wines
in the right hand column.
Draw a line from the food to the wine … The answers are on page 95.

Asparagus	Muscadet
Christmas Pudding	German Riesling Kabinett
Consomme	Sancerre
Fois Gras	Champagne
Fruits de Mers	Sauvignon Blanc
Goat's Cheese	Sauternes
Oysters	Beaujolais
Parma Ham and Melon	Sauternes
Roast Lamb	Port
Roast Pork	Sweet Vouvray
Roquefort	Pinot Grigio
Stilton	Fino Sherry
Strawberries and Cream	Liqueur Muscat
Sushi	Red Bordeaux

Some red wines are best enjoyed with beef or lamb...

...and others are perfect with chocolates, magazines and a sloppy Labrador...

Speech bubble: What about this Chardonnay, Mum?

Speech bubble: No-too buttery... Aha! This Berry Bros. Sauvignon is light and refreshing - that should fit the bill...

Speech bubble: ...mmm...the perfect compliment to a box of choccies and a romantic comedy...

WINE QUIZ

Do you know your Bordeaux from your Burgundy? How long should one chill the Veuve Clicquot? (Daffy's not fussy as long as her glass is full.) Find out if you need to brush up your wine knowledge. Pit your wits against a partner or play solo (with a glass of something to hand to keep you company). The only lifelines here are 'phone a friend' or 'pour another glass'. Answers are on page 95.

① What is the normal alcohol percentage for sherry?

★ 5–7%
★ 8–14%
★ 15–20%
★ 21% or more

② Which of the following is not a South African wine producing region?

★ Stellenbosch
★ Olifantsrivier
★ Constantia
★ Mendocino

③ In which country is the River Spey?

★ Portugal
★ Scotland
★ Mexico
★ Denmark

④ Where is the wine growing region Stellenbosch?

★ Australia
★ New Zealand
★ South Africa
★ Germany

⑤ From which country does the Allegrini brand originate?

★ Spain
★ France
★ Portugal
★ Italy

⑥ What is the recommended serving temperature for Champagne?

★ 0–5 Centigrade
★ 5–10 Centigrade
★ 10–15 Centigrade

⑦ Neusiederlersee (a region that produces dessert wines) is in which country?

★ Hungary
★ Switzerland
★ Germany
★ Austria

⑧ Which of the following was the best vintage for Chablis?

★ 1980
★ 1991
★ 1994
★ 1996

⑨ Penfolds Grange is made from?

★ Cabernet Sauvignon
★ Merlot and Cabernet Sauvignon
★ Terra Rosso
★ Shiraz and Cabernet Sauvignon

⑩ In which region in France is Muscat Beaumes de Venise made?

★ Rhône
★ Burgundy
★ Loire
★ Cognac

⑪ Which is the only firm to ferment and mature all its Champagne in small oak casks?

★ Krug
★ Veuve Clicquot
★ Louis Roederer
★ Bollinger

⑫ In 1985 which illustrious St. Emilion property was stripped of its 1er Grand Cru Classé status?

★ Château Beausèjour-Duffau
★ Château Cheval Blanc
★ Château Beausèjour-Bécot
★ Château Figeac

⑬ Which of the following red wines should be chilled?

★ Bordeaux
★ Beaujolais
★ Rioja
★ Australian Shiraz

⑭ What is known as a Marie-Jeanne?

★ A 2.25 litre bottle from Bordeaux
★ A French giant baguette
★ A non-vintage Brut Champagne
★ A East German tennis player

⑮ Who introduced vines to England?

★ Greeks
★ Romans
★ Vikings
★ Spanish

⑯ What do crystals in the bottom of a bottle indicate?

★ Wine past maturity
★ Contaminated wine
★ High-quality wine making

"Frankly, no - I wouldn't like baked bean flavoured crisps with my Petrus '82..."

"Let's have a look - Yup - it's definitely red wine..."

"Aah, yes - a heady bouquet of dry rot and wet labrador..."

This wine needs to be given the chance to breathe...

Heavens! Does it?..

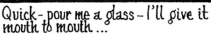

Quick - pour me a glass - I'll give it mouth to mouth...

⑰ The white grape Furmint blended with Harslevelu, and sometimes Muscat, produces which famous sweet wine?

★ Coteaux de Layon
★ Muscat de Beaumes de Venise
★ Barsac
★ Tokaji Aszu

⑱ Cloudy Bay Sauvignon Blanc is from which country?

★ Italy
★ Australia
★ United States
★ New Zealand

⑲ The Pinot Noir grape is the dominant force in producing the red wines of Bordeaux?

★ True
★ False

⑳ In which French wine region is Minervois made?

★ Loire Valley
★ Bulgaria
★ Languedoc
★ Rhône Valley

Answers are on page 95. Give yourself one point for every correct answer.

If you scored 19 and over
Dicky would be proud to spend an evening showing you his wine cellar and asking your opinion on some of his finest vintages.

If you scored between 11–18
Not bad. You clearly care more than just drinking the stuff but if you did a bit more homework you would soon be able to hold your head up high with Dicky and his pals.

If you scored between 4–10
Oh dear, 'could do better'. You clearly choose your wine by price. If you don't wish to be known by the sobriquet of 'you know who' one suggests you brush up your knowledge a bit before your next visit to Tottering Hall. The nice people at Berry Bros. & Rudd will spare your blushes if you enrol on one of their wine knowledge courses.

If you scored less than 3
How many glasses have you had?

'Thanks to Berry Bros. & Rudd for providing the quiz!'

THE MALE CHARACTER...

A tendency to lay down the law...

...and then accept amendments...

THE FEMALE CHARACTER: The prudence to reach for a chair and a drink before answering the telephone...

THE LABRADOR CHARACTER: Always at his master's heel...

40

Lady Daffy Tottering

Tottering Hall
Tottering-by-Gently
North Pimmshire
Phone (00) 666-1234
daffy@tottering.com

[insert date here]

[template],
Address line 1
Address line 2

Dear [template],

It was so nice / unexpected / revealing / amusing [delete as appropriate] to make your acquaintance / see you again / endure the pleasure of your company / realise that we have nothing in common [delete as appropriate].

I/we [delete as appropriate] haven't had more small talk / stress / entertainment / sex [delete as appropriate] for a long time and I/we [delete as appropriate] hope that I/we [delete as appropriate] can do it again soon / forgive and forget / persuade you to emigrate / impose myself/ourselves [delete as appropriate] on YOU one day.

May I/we [delete as appropriate] say what a delight / an insight / a drudge [delete as appropriate] it was for me/us [delete as appropriate] to have you to help consume our vintage reserves / to stay / to wait on hand and foot [delete as appropriate].

Please do feel free to come again / keep going / petition in vain [delete as appropriate] if you're ever divorced / in the area / prepared to replace the wine consumed [delete as appropriate].

Sincerely,

[template]

TOTTERING LEADERGRAM

In a Leadergram puzzle the answers to the clues are inserted in the numbered squares in the Clues grid opposite, then the individual letters of the answer are transferred to the similarly numbered squares in the main Grid on page 44.

The first column of the answers on the Clues grid shows a book title and the name of the author. When the puzzle is completed correctly the main Grid will reveal a quotation from that work, ignoring punctuation.

THE GUEST FROM HELL

Clues

1. A type of country cottage (8)

2. A bygone school subject (7)

3. Over-enthusiastically gushing (10)

4. Discharges from a mucous surface (6)

5. Non-humorous (7)

6. A compass point (4)

7. Abbreviated glasses (5)

8. Inconsiderate (11)

9. Programmed (9)

10. Dashing flier? (7)

11. Cleaned too thoroughly (10)

12. Hindu instructor (9)

13. A group under the same roof (9)

14. Steplike arrangement (7)

15. Used in chemical warfare (8)

16. A means of escape (8)

17. A stupid person (9)

18. Excited exclamation (5)

19. Artistic (9)

20. However (9)

21. Notoriously bad (8)

22. Moves back and forth (8)

23. Tickle (9)

24. Queen Victoria was not! (6)

25. Early Peruvians (5)

26. Rear ends (5)

27. Display place (8)

28. Ornamental gypsum (9)

29. Fashionable (6)

30. Involved in the formation of starch (8)

31. Sullied (8)

32. Curses (5)

33. Many (8)

1.	166 T	78	28	214	75	39	184	29		
2.	240 H	145	58	110	37	140	64			
3.	34 E	9	35	191	163	5	113	26	183	15
4.	235 G	127	92	197	33	200				
5.	74 U	57	120	232	72	242	186			
6.	3 E	234	41	137						
7.	237 S	77	61	14	83					
8.	244 T	124	94	188	17	76	21	11	228	109	7
9.	4 F	227	27	170	241	51	245	135	45	
10.	174 R	117	95	116	125	221	168			
11.	68 O	103	82	115	90	10	126	201	112	70
12.	196 M	50	179	32	233	30	85	101	169	
13.	198 H	231	108	220	154	141	136	69	144	
14.	250 E	194	158	66	182	219	111			
15.	161 L	172	62	40	176	128	247	114		
16.	118 L	59	122	129	150	131	211	139		
17.	65 B	192	177	189	208	49	175	13	185	
18.	165 Y	16	52	195	187					
19.	142 A	104	149	1	67	106	99	181	230	
20.	12 L	225	243	20	133	88	54	155	19	
21.	43 I	132	146	173	22	97	18	81		
22.	130 S	2	23	48	93	224	71	217		
23.	153 T	46	25	246	119	204	80	8	91	
24.	84 A	42	248	213	199	162				
25.	56 I	143	31	102	24					
26.	6 R	238	105	216	47					
27.	157 S	86	151	171	36	100	159	38		
28.	210 A	212	63	223	207	73	226	209	121	
29.	107 M	202	249	148	55	138				
30.	218 P	96	180	53	44	190	222	205		
31.	89 S	60	98	206	239	147	236	193		
32.	87 O	164	178	134	152					
33.	229 N	160	123	215	79	167	203	156		

Grid

Position each letter revealed by the clues according to its number in the Clues grid on page 43 in the corresponding numbered box below. We have given you a head start by positioning the ones already revealed in the Clues grid on the previous page. Once all the letters are complete you will be able to read the phrase.

1	2	3 E	4 F	5	6 R	7	8	9	10	11	12 L	13	14	15	16	17	18	19	20	21	22	23	24	25
26	27	28	29	30	31	32	33	34 E	35	36	37	38	39	40	41	42	43 I	44	45	46	47	48	49	50
51	52	53	54	55	56 I	57	58	59	60	61	62	63	64	65 B	66	67	68 O	69	70	71	72	73	74 U	75
76	77	78	79	80	81	82	83	84 A	85	86	87 O	88	89 S	90	91	92	93	94	95	96	97	98	99	100
101	102	103	104	105	106	107 M	108	109	110	111	112	113	114	115	116	117	118 L	119	120	121	122	123	124	125
126	127	128	129	130 S	131	132	133	134	135	136	137	138	139	140	141	142 A	143	144	145	146	147	148	149	150
151	152	153 T	154	155	156	157 S	158	159	160	161 L	162	163	164	165 Y	166 T	167	168	169	170	171	172	173	174 R	175
176	177	178	179	180	181	182	183	184	185	186	187	188	189	190	191	192	193	194	195	196 M	197	198 H	199	200
201	202	203	204	205	206	207	208	209	210 A	211	212	213	214	215	216	217	218 P	219	220	221	222	223	224	225
226	227	228	229 N	230	231	232	233	234	235 G	236	237 S	238	239	240 H	241	242	243	244 T	245	246	247	248	249	250 E

Once revealed write out the final phrase here
(and check your answer on page 96).

"No, darling–I can't invite the Crepuscula-Harflytes – there's far too much risk of being invited back...."

The departure of a weekend guest who didn't leave by four on Sunday...

"3rd Tuesday of the 5th month - is that this pink bin with purple spots for Champagne corks and take away curry containers only?.."

Well, that's what Allan told me!

Daffy! Stop spreading gossip!

I'm not gossiping, Dicky - I'm recycling information...

My husband ran off with another woman so I divorced him...she's welcome to him.

Oh! Well done! I suppose it's what the government's encouraging us all to do...

...recycle our household waste...

Where is this recycling of household waste going to stop?..

47

JOIN THE DOTS: DAFFY

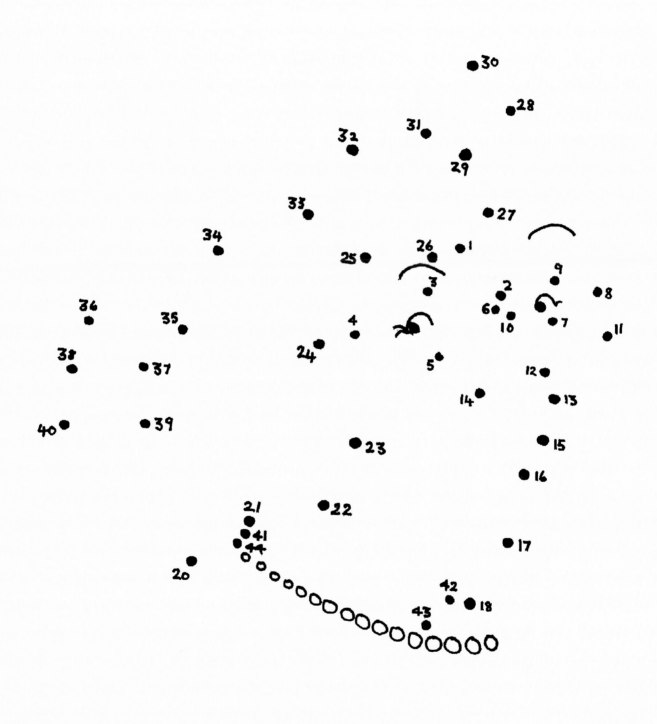

JOIN THE DOTS: DICKY

SUDOKU WITH A TWIST

A sudoku puzzle is always made up of 9 numbers… Each row, each column and each of the 3x3 boxes must contain each of the numbers 1 to 9. However, 'Tottering sudoku' has an extra twist to keep you on your toes.

Each of the Tottering characters on the right represents a number from 1 to 9. Your task is to identify which number goes with which character (you can write them in the line under each portrait) as well as complete the Sudoku puzzles – one is at Daffy's level (easy) and the other is at Dicky's (difficult)!

If you need a bit of help take a quick peep at the key on page 96 and then try and solve the puzzles. The answers to both puzzles are on page 96.

Lord Tottering 'Dicky'

Lady Tottering 'Daffy'

Serena

Freddy

Gladys Shagpile

Daisy

Slobber

Scribble

Hon Jon

Daffy's Puzzle

Dicky's Puzzle

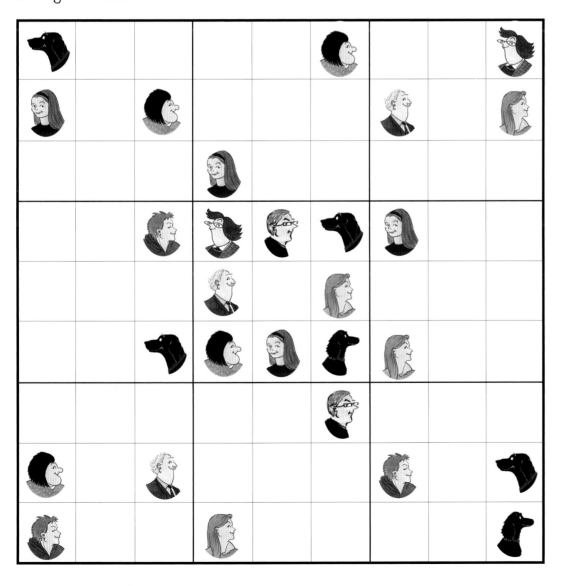

A WOMAN'S PRAYER

Now I lay me down to sleep,
I pray the Lord my shape to keep,
Please, no wrinkles… please, no bags
And please lift my bum before it sags.
Please, no age spots… please no grey
And as for my belly… please take it away.
Please keep me healthy, please keep me young
And thank you dear Lord, for all that you have done.

Couldn't you choose something else to read at bedtime, darling?..

HAZARDOUS MATERIALS
DATA SHEET

CHEMICAL NAME
FEMTEX

ANALYSIS
ELEMENT: WOMAN
SYMBOL: WO
DISCOVERER: ADAM
ATOMIC MASS: ACCEPTED AS 55KG, BUT KNOWN TO VARY FROM
               45KG TO 225KG
OCCURRENCE: FOUND IN LARGE QUANTITIES IN URBAN AREAS
               WITH TRACE ELEMENTS IN OUTLYING REGIONS.

PHYSICAL PROPERTIES
1. SURFACE NORMALLY COVERED WITH YOGHURT AND CUCUMBER.
2. BOILS AT ABSOLUTELY NOTHING, FREEZES FOR NO APPARENT REASON.
3. MELTS IF GIVEN SPECIAL TREATMENT.
4. BITTER IF USED INCORRECTLY.
5. FOUND IN VARIOUS GRADES RANGING FROM VIRGIN MATERIAL TO COMMON ORE.
6. YIELDS TO PRESSURE IF EXPERTLY APPLIED.

CHEMICAL PROPERTIES
1. AFFINITY TO GOLD, SILVER, PLATINUM AND ALL PRECIOUS STONES.
2. ABSORBS GREAT QUANTITIES OF EXPENSIVE SUBSTANCES.
3. EXPLODES SPONTANEOUSLY WITHOUT APPARENT REASON OR WARNING.
4. GREATLY INCREASED ACTIVITY WHEN SATURATED WITH ALCOHOL.
5. THE MOST POWERFUL MONEY REDUCING AGENT KNOWN TO MAN.

COMMON USE
1. HIGHLY ORNAMENTAL, ESPECIALLY IN SPORTS CARS.
2. CAN BE A GREAT AID TO RELAXATION.
3. CAN BE AN EFFECTIVE CLEANING AGENT.

TESTS
1. PURE SPECIMENS TURN BRIGHT PINK WHEN FOUND IN THEIR NATURAL STATE.
2. TURNS GREEN WHEN PLACED ALONGSIDE A SUPERIOR SPECIMEN.

HAZARDS
1. HIGHLY DANGEROUS EXCEPT IN EXPERIENCED HANDS.
2. ILLEGAL TO POSSESS MORE THAN ONE, ALTHOUGH SEVERAL CAN BE MAINTAINED AT DIFFERENT LOCATIONS AS LONG AS SPECIMENS DO NOT COME IN DIRECT CONTACT WITH EACH OTHER.

"FEMTEX"

An oestrogen charged weapon that is unstable and can explode at a second's notice...

IN TIMES OF STRESS . . .

Grant me the serenity to
accept the things I cannot change
The courage to change
things I cannot accept
And the wisdom to hide
The bodies of those I had to
kill today
Because they got on my nerves.

Also help me to be careful
of the toes I step on today
As they may be connected
To the feet I have to kiss
tomorrow.

Help me always to give 100%...
12% on Monday
23% on Tuesday
40% on Wednesday
20% on Thursday
and
5% on Friday...

And help me to remember...
...When I'm having a bad day
And it seems that people
Are trying to wind me up...

That it takes 42 muscles to frown.
and
only 28 to smile...

(...but using more muscles burns more calories...)

Dear Lord - I pray for wisdom to understand my family...

Love to forgive them, and patience for their inability to understand the purpose of a dishwasher. Because Lord, if I pray for strength...

... I will beat them to a pulp...

A woman's life can feel like performing a juggling act whilst riding a unicycle through a ploughed field...

Sometimes we just have to prioritise...

QUIET MY MIND... **Ow! My back is killing me!** QUIET... PEACEFUL THOUGHTS... I DO NOT WANT CHOCOLATE... I DO NOT WANT CHOCOLATE...

SINKING INTO A DEEP, PEACEFUL STATE OF RESTFUL ALERTNESS... **Damn! I forgot to pick up the dry cleaning**... I DO NOT WANT CHOCOLATE ANY MORE...

SCRITCH!
SCRATCH!

I now NEED it.

TRA!LA!
PING!
TRA!!LA!
PING!

HORMONES...

Severe hormone warning: Localised heavy outbursts of unpredictable behaviour...

Foggy thinking with Temperatures fluctuating in the mid 50's...

Changeable with some stroppy spells...

Light and sunny all day throughout the house...

TOTTERING JAM

Raspberry Jam

4lbs raspberries
4lbs preserving sugar
Knob of butter

Put the raspberries in jam saucepan & simmer,
stirring occasionally, for 20 mins.
Take off heat & add sugar stirring until dissolved
Add knob of butter & boil rapidly for half an hour.
Test for set. Stand for 15 mins. Pot.

Strawberry Jam

3½ lbs strawbs
3 tbsp. lemon juice
3 lbs preserving sugar
Knob butter.

Put strawbs in pan with lemon juice & simmer,
stirring occasionally for 25 mins. Take off heat &
add sugar. Stir until dissolved. Add butter &
bring to boil rapidly for 20 mins
Test for set. Stand for 15 mins. Pot.

" My quack tells me there's nothing he can give me to stop me having any more grandchildren..."

Imagine if children were like vintage wines, James...

You could store them away in the cellar for twenty years...

...and they'd reach maturity all on their own...

My son has invited me out there, but I can't go, you see, because of my dogs...

Then he says - 'who's more important - the dogs or your own grandchildren?'...

I hope you told him....

The dream...

The reality...

BUILD YOUR OWN STEALTH BOMBER

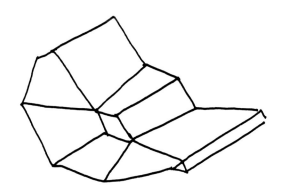

Take your time to fold this carefully and this bomber will reward you with long smooth glides.

TIPS

- Photocopy the template page opposite and practise folding this marked up sheet first until you are familiar with the instructions. Then you can use an unmarked sheet or trace lightly over the template with a pencil so the marks can be rubbed out later.
- Make sure your paper is trimmed to the exact size of the template. With the paper in the 'Up' orientation you want the top of fold marks 1 and 2 to end directly in their respective corners.
- If you want a larger or smaller aeroplane just adjust the size of the template on a photocopier accordingly, keeping everything in proportion.

STEP 1
Orientate the template with the 'up' arrow at the top of the page. Then, flip the paper over so that you cannot see any of the fold lines.

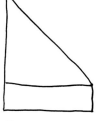

STEP 2
Fold the top right corner down and to the left until fold line 1 appears and crease along dotted line.

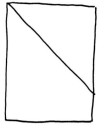

STEP 3
Unfold the fold you have just created.

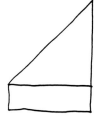

STEP 4
Repeat the procedure above by folding the top left corner down and to the right. Make a crease along fold line 2.

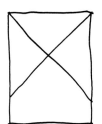

STEP 5
Unfold the fold you have just created.

STEP 6
This step is a bit tricky. Lift the left and right edges of the paper and push them toward each other while folding the top triangle on to the bottom one. This will make a crease along fold lines 3 so that you end up with the shape below.

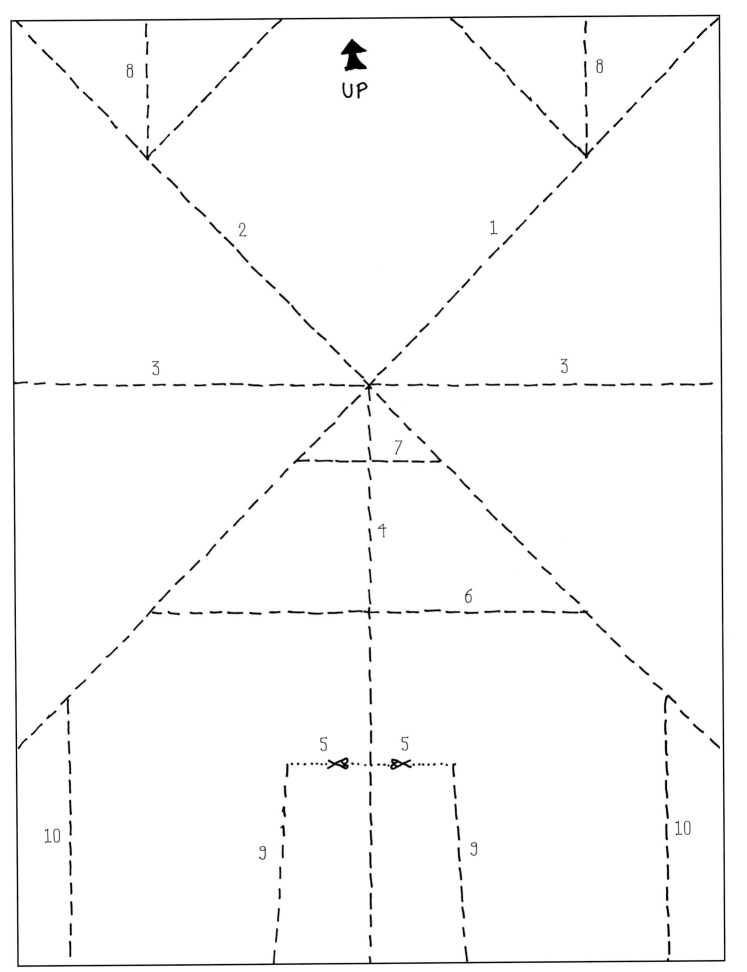

UP

8   8

2   1

3   3

7

4

6

5   5

10   10

9   9

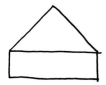

STEP 7

You should now have this shape.

STEP 8

Fold the right side over on to the left side along fold line 4. Cut along the dotted cut line 5.

STEP 9

Unfold so it looks like this.

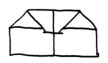

STEP 10

Fold the top point over and crease along fold line 6. Tuck the nose into the slit you cut along line 5.

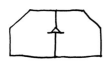

STEP 11

Flip the paper over and fold the nose up along fold line 7.

vertical fold line

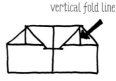

STEP 12

Flip the paper back cover again. Fold the top layer only of the triangle-shaped flaps in along the vertical fold line 8.

pocket

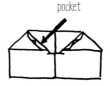

STEP 13

Tuck the flaps into the pockets near the nose of the plane. (Note: the 'flaps' are the top layer you have just folded in Step 12.)
Take the tip of the triangle and push it into the pocket so the complete triangle is tucked in neatly. Repeat for the other side.

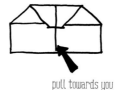

pull towards you

STEP 14

You should now see this shape. Locate the crease below cut line 5. Lift and pull this crease carefully towards you at the same as you are folding the plane in half towards you. Be warned! It is very easy to pull too hard and tear the opening so take your time! This will create creases along fold lines 9.

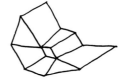

STEP 15

Partially unfold the fold you just created. You should now have this shape.

STEP 16

Fold down the winglets along fold lines 10. Now you are ready to fly!

Hold the plane with your thumb against the nose and your index and middle finger behind cut line 5.

Launch very gently from above your head . . . and watch it fly . . .

Dicky suggests decorating your plane with the traditional RAF logo for greater authenticity.

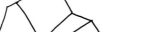

DICKY'S PAPER AEROPLANE FACTS

A paper plane is sometimes called an aerogami, after the origami (the Japanese art of paper folding).

Leonardo da Vinci (1452-1519) is often credited as the inventor of the paper plane but it is more likely that the credit is due to the Chinese, since they had invented both paper and the kite as long as 3000 years ago. However Leonardo does refer to making a model plane out of parchment – parchment, made out of thin animal skin, was the nearest thing to paper at that time.

The most accepted version of the creation of the paper aeroplane as we know it today was in 1930 by Jack Northrop. Northrop used paper planes to test his ideas for flying real-life aircraft.

DAFFY'S CRAB APPLE MINT JELLY

This is an old family recipe that is a firm favourite for Sunday lunch …. One whole jam jar usually gets guzzled every time roast lamb is put on the table.

Not only is it really good but it is dead easy too. I love it that you don't have to peel or core the apples so, although it takes a couple of days because of the straining and slow cooking, it is actually labour free!

You will need:
3lb 5oz crab apples
1oz fresh mint leaves
1 cinnamon stick
$1\frac{1}{4}$ pints cold water
$3\frac{1}{2}$oz baby spinach (yes, spinach... optional but good)
10 fl oz cider vinegar (other will do)
preserving sugar

1. Gather your crab apples from the garden (windfalls are fine). Wash (don't bother to core and peel them) and cut into smallish pieces. Put into a slow cooker with a quarter of the mint leaves, the cinnamon stick and water. Leave on low overnight until the apples go pulpy and collapse into a mush.

2. Add spinach and vinegar and cook, uncovered, for 15 minutes.

3. Leave to strain through a jelly bag (you can abandon this for a good day or night...).

4. Wrap remaining mint in a muslin bag or similar.

5. Measure juice and place in a saucepan with 1lb 2oz sugar per pint of juice.

6. Place pan over a medium heat to dissolve the sugar.

7. Add the mint and boil rapidly for 10 minutes.

8. Test for set by placing a small amount on a cold saucer. Let it cool for about a minute and stick your finger in it – if wrinkles form on the surface of the blob as you push, you have set!

9. When it is ready, using a funnel and a very fine wire sieve, carefully pour the liquid into sterilized jars. I sometimes use two sieves to make sure that the jelly going into the jars is absolutely clear of any pieces of mint.

Cover the jars with greaseproof paper and leave until cool. Seal with clean and dry lids. Label and date.

Now go and breed some lambs …

TEENAGE FACTS : They will spontaneously combust and cease to exist if disconnected from cyberspace...

Good morning, Grandpa!

Ah! Freddy! The resident Jeeves...

...with a mug of tepid bath water garnished with a drowned spider...

I didn't even know there WAS a camera in my mobile phone...

All phones have them! Look! You've taken loads of pictures...

...but they all seem to be of the inside of your Husky pocket...

Does young Freddy want some casual work in the hols this year, Daffy?

Thats very sweet of you, Bunty, but he'll probably want to stick with his usual holiday job...

...eating me out of house and home and going round the house putting all the loo seats up...

What do you mean: "What's for lunch"? It's 2 o'clock in the afternoon! If you wanted lunch you should have got out of bed sooner...

It's not my fault. You wouldn't be able to get up in time either if you were a teenager...

...It's very tiring staying up 'till 4 a.m. chatting on the internet to all your friends...

Me-cum om-nes plan-gi-te! - Ooh! That top B flats hard...

I have to practise singing my soprano part for Carmina Burana...

But that's not singing, Granny - that's child abuse...

SPOT THE DIFFERENCE

Can you find ten differences in Daffy's 'Swiss Army Barbour'? Answers are on page 96.

THE PLEASURE OF GARDENING...

...Being pricked by thorny things...

THE PLEASURE OF GARDENING...

...Being stung by stinging things...

THE PLEASURE OF GARDENING...

...Being stuck to by sticky things...

THE PLEASURE OF GARDENING...

...Being bitten by buzzy things...

Our first organic carrot, Dicky...

If any of the experiences below seem alarmingly familiar then perhaps
you are in need of some Tottering Brain Training . . .

WHAT DOES DAFFY HAVE IN HER HANDBAG?

Play 'Daffy's Game' to find out.

'Daffy's Game' is a Tottering version of that old nursery favourite 'Kim's Game'.
You can play this with two or more people or by yourself against the clock.

Take 30 seconds (or adjust time according to youth, senility or level of alcohol
consumption) to look at the contents of Daffy's handbag below … Then close
the book and write down on a piece of paper as many of the items as you can
remember within a previously agreed allotted time (for example, 1 minute).

If you are playing as a group you can either, all look and write at the same time
or, if you are playing with handicaps to accommodate youth, senility or alcohol
consumption, take it in turns. The person with the highest number of correct
answers wins. In the event of a tiebreak the person who finished first wins.
Total number of objects to find is 22.

"To my deafness I'm accustomed,
to my dentures I'm resigned,
I can manage my bifocals,
But oh! How I miss my mind…"

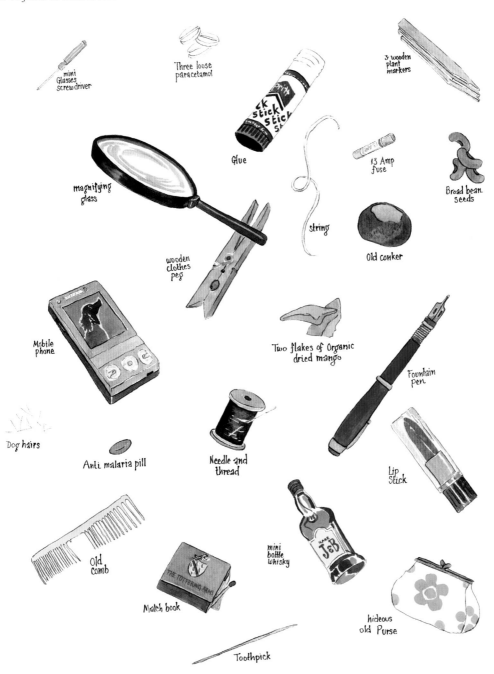

mini
Glasses
screwdriver

Three loose
paracetamol

Glue

3 wooden
plant
markers

magnifying
glass

string

13 Amp
fuse

Broad bean
seeds

Old conker

wooden
clothes
peg

Mobile
phone

Two flakes of Organic
dried mango

Fountain
Pen

Dog hairs

Anti malaria pill

Needle and
thread

Lip
Stick

Old
comb

Match book

mini
bottle
whisky

hideous
old Purse

Toothpick

TOTTERING CROSSWORD

ACROSS CLUES

1. Is Tottering putting up a false front? (5)
3. None of Daffy's (sober) fear Dicky. (9)
8. With 19, family home is staggering. (9)
10. Examine closely Daffy's breakfast offering. (5)
11. Little reward in remit for new building. (5)
12. Letting men go from poor housing Dicky's holding? (5)
14. In recess (for Freddy?) — mushy peas. (4)
15. Spurious alibi 'a cold', – that's outrageous! (10)
18. Lose one's balance? Slips do heal in a disc. (2,8)
19. Ancient seat could be a bit of a drag, we hear (4)
21. Tottering Hall wants concession for exhibition (5)
23. 'Eden's Hybrid' are what's lacking (5)
25. Xanthine is the colour of what's in Dotty's dry martini (5)
26. Is duck one excuse for Daffy taking to gin? (9)
28. Such relics as Gladys? (9)
29. Pimmshire flower-girl? (5)

DOWN CLUES

1 & 24. Lady friend spotted with skin problem has a pet (5,5-4)
2. Operate boycott (3)
3. Decent hearing for Aunt Sally, perhaps? (4,5)
4. Appropriate party for the Totterings? (5)
5. Much disliked captain takes aboard unknown man for situation of 8 ac. (2-6)
6. Upper-class actors? I star in play (11)
7 & 2. Smooth short smoke for Daffy? (4,3)
9. The noble next to Dicky, almost ahead. (4)
11. Obedient servant, Mistress takes a nap twice. (3,8)
13. The long adherence Dicky has for Pratts? (3,7)
16. Tenners are curses without the Windsor possibly. (9)
17. Edging along the Hall roof, soldier takes step back (8)
20. Rank Honjon may live to see? (4)
22. Ivory one wrote about. (5)
24. Name of 1 d's solicitor. (4)
27. Gone away. (3)

(Answers are on page 96)

The answer to number thirteen across is 'INFURIATING'...

TOTTERING CHRISTMAS RECIPES

TOTTERING TODDY

1 oz. Port wine (25g)
1 Pint fresh green tea (550ml)
4 oz. Sugar (110g)
Peel of 1 Lemon
1 glass of Brandy
1 bottle Scotch Whisky

Heat and serve piping hot!

Ale Flip

Beat separately 2 egg whites and 4 yolks. Combine them, adding 4 tablespoons of moistened sugar and 1/2 nutmeg grated. Put 1 quart ale in a saucepan and bring to the boil. Pour in the egg-sugar mixture, gradually, stirring as you add. Transfer the steaming result to a robust pitcher and pour back and forth rapidly between this pitcher and its twin brother, each time holding the pourer high above the receiver, until a handsome froth is attained.

Serve in mugs or large goblets. One pillow to every customer.

Christmas Rum Punch

6 oranges
1/2 gallon sweet cider
1 bottle Jamaica rum, bestest
sugar to taste
whole cloves
ground cinammon and nutmeg

Stick the oranges full of cloves and bake them in the oven until they soften. Place oranges in the punch bowl, pour over the rum and add granulated sugar to taste. Set fire to rum and in a few minutes add the cider slowly to extinguish the flame. Stir in cinammon and nutmeg, and keep the mixture hot.

MRS SHAGPILE'S THRIFTY TIPS

A child's pushchair with a basket strapped into it makes
an excellent vehicle for bringing logs or coal buckets into the
drawing room fire.

Before throwing away worn rubber gloves,
cut strips from the cuffs which will make
some strong and useful elastic bands.

To clear the stains from narrow-necked vases,
use a proprietary brand of loo cleaner,
diluted with a little water. Allow to stand and
rinse out very thoroughly before further use.

The slight burn marks on carpets caused by sparks
from open fires can often be removed by rubbing
vigorously with the cut surface of an onion.

Gladys Shagpile.

Clean ivory piano keys with a little toothpaste on a
damp cloth. 'Rinse' with milk and polish off with a soft cloth.

To make your candles burn longer, place in the deep freeze for a few hours before use.

New nylon stockings and tights will have their life greatly prolonged by a
night in the deep freeze. Rinse in warm water, squeeze out gently, secure in a
plastic bag and place in the freezer or ice-making compartment of the fridge.
Next day, thaw out and hang to dry.

All them expensive hair gels are a con - marmalade is much cheaper
but you've got to be careful of wasps in the summer...

You've started smoking again, Mrs Shagpile!

It's to help get me fitter - the doctor told me to do it...

He said I had to take up slowly doing something that makes me just slightly out of breath two or three times a week...

Ah! Morning, Mrs Shagpile - scrubbing the floors in my wine cellars, are you!

Yes - I'm well into my spring cleaning, Lord T...

...and I've had every one of these dusty old bottles out and given them a good soap down in my bucket...

Gabble, gabble, gabble! You'd think them politicians would 'ave better things to talk about...

Like what, Mrs Shagpile?

My poor old feet, for a start...

75

THE PERILS OF GETTING OLD

You really are getting old, Dicky Tottering...

What makes you suddenly say that?

I saw you look at the menu before the waitress...

I've lost the damn telephone! I've searched in all the obvious places!

Well, why don't you try in the fridge or the oven, then?

I told you! I've already searched in all the *OBVIOUS* places...

...We never had even the tiniest conflict for years...

...then - completely unprovoked. -

Gravity turned nasty on me...

76

ME AND MY VITAMINS...
I take them to keep me young, thin and beautiful...

Being a woman over 50 brings so many demands on ones time just for basic maintenance - if it's not flabby arms it's the pelvic floor...

...let alone the hours spent searching for handbags and specs because of failing eyes and memory...

Woops! Must go - my roots need redoing...

There's nothing worse than being stuck in a bloody traffic jam!..

Oh! There is for a woman...

...being stuck inside a car with a man stuck in a traffic jam...

Daffy! What on earth are you doing! That's the second red light we've gone straight through!

Sorry, darling - I was just distracted for a second listening to Womans Hour...

... I thought you were driving...

Right! Stop! We've all got to pull together!

... work as a team...

...and do it MY way...

"You'll have to back up - I don't do reverse..."

Oh! No! That's all we need! That man in front is wearing a hat...

We'll be *really* late now...

...men in hats drive 30 miles per hour slower than anyone else on the road...

If you don't zero your mileometer after filling up, how are you going to work out how many miles you're getting to the gallon...

Women don't go in for pointless arithmatic like that... I mean where would it end?..

...sitting timing how many hours I'm getting per light bulb?..

THE PERFECT MARRIAGE

Being supportive...

making time to listen to each other...

dealing with problems together...

keeping active in the bed department...

ENJOYING ONE'S HUSBAND'S HOBBIES...

ENJOYING ONES WIFES HOBBIES...

MY FRIEND

There is nothing so pleasant
as walking alone
with a friend in the forest,
though you're miles from home.

It's that feeling of peace
in the womb before birth;
togetherness! There's
nothing else like it on earth.

We walk on grass matting,
the trees seem to call,
but it's only the breeze --
blowing gently -- that's all.

And my friend seems so happy
as he talks to me -- Oh!
how I wish I could understand,
Please! Let it be so!

We're going deeper now,
far, through this fabulous green,
there are colours in here
more than I've ever seen.

But where is my friend?
he must have walked on.
I only stopped for a moment,
oh, where can he have gone?

I'm running through the bracken now,
searching in vain,
I can't see him anywhere,
I must try again.

Help me to find him,
please God? If you're there.
I'm desperate to find him,
just tell me where!

Ah! There he is now,
thank God! He's alright.
But he shouldn't run off like that,
I had such a fright.

Still, he's glad that I've found him
put an end to my grief,
so I bark, give a whine,
and wag my tail with relief.

Anonywoof

THINGS TO DO IN THE GARDEN WITHOUT GARDENING ...

"You dowse for drains if you like - I'm off in search of the fountain of youth...."

What a perfect day! The sun is out and so are the kids...

That's an awfully risky shot to take so early in the weekend...

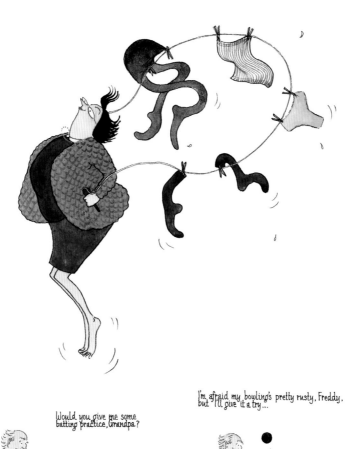

Would you give me some batting practice, Grandpa?

I'm afraid my bowling's pretty rusty, Freddy, but I'll give it a try...

Just stick to underarm then — I won't tell your friends...

Wimbledon

5 REASONS WHY COMPUTERS MUST BE MALE...

1. They're heavily dependent on external tools and equipment.
2. They periodically cut you off, just when you think you've established a connection.
3. They usually do what you ask them to do, but they won't do more than they have to and they won't think of it on their own.
4. They're typically obsolete within five years and need to be traded in for a new model. Some users, however, feel they've already invested so much in the machine that they struggle on with an underpowered system.
5. The only time you have their attention is when you turn them on.

A PRAYER FOR THE TECHNICALLY-CHALLENGED

Our program, who are in Memory,
Hello be thy name.
Thy operating system come,
Thy commands be done,
At the Printer as they are on the screen.

Give us this day our daily data,
And forgive us our input errors as we forgive those
whose logic circuits are faulty.

Lead us not into frustration,
And deliver us from power surges.
For thine is the Algorithm,
The Application,
And the Solution,
Looping for ever and ever.

AMSN.com

5 REASONS WHY COMPUTERS MUST BE FEMALE...

1. No one but their creator understands their internal logic.
2. Even your smallest mistakes are immediately committed to memory for future reference.
3. The native language used to communicate with other computers is incomprehensible.
4. The message 'bad command or filename' is about as informative as 'if you don't know why I'm furious with you – I'm certainly not going to tell you!'
5. As soon as you make a commitment to one, you find yourself spending every spare penny on accessories for it.

This computer seems to have siezed up - I can't get it to go at all...

I don't think I can help - I don't know the first thing about them...

...when did you last change the oil?

There's a thing here saying we've got mail, Dicky...

That's odd - it's only ten past nine...

The postman never usually gets here before eleven...

I thought I'd just have a go on your computer, Freddy - but it seems to be on the blink...it won't work...

That's because the mouse is down here on the floor, Granny...

Oh! I thought that was the foot pedal...

TOTTERING WORD CHAIN

How quickly can you transform Daffy into Dicky by changing only one letter at a time?
No nonsense words please! See if you can beat 13 moves… The answer is on page 96.

....

....

....

....

....

....

THE MALE AND FEMALE CHARACTERS

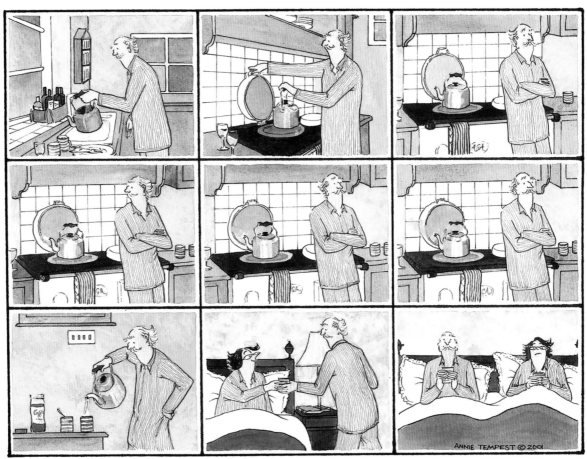

He makes coffee...

She makes coffee...

Why do you keep asking my opinion over all these things?..

...I know perfectly well that whatever I say is going to be wrong...

No, it's not...

Just simmer down, Daffy...

I was only trying to help...

Well don't! Being calm and logical is never helpful to a cross wife...

You said 'I feel fat and ugly' and I said 'I'm sure you do'...

So why are you looking at me like that?...

I was trying to 'validate your feelings' which is what you keep asking me to do...

90

1 Kg equals 2.2 lbs - 14 lbs in a stone - 16 oz in a pound - thats 41.37 of the 2 kg bags of sugar...

You see - the scales are working perfectly...

Dicky? I'm completely lost...

OK, OK - calm down, Daffy...

Now. Where exactly are you?

I'm turning into an amorphous lump on top of skinny legs -

Most men would take that as a cue to pay their wife a much needed compliment..

Your eyesight is excellent, dear...

Would you know where your wife keeps the sugar bowl?

No. Not the foggiest idea, I'm afraid ...

Nor me - we must stick together - we're an endangered species, you know...

Is this your bag and did you pack it yourself, Sir?

In answer to your first question - yes, it is my suitcase ...

...and to your second, no - don't be ridiculous - of course I didn't pack it myself...

Is that the shop? Yes, my wife Daffy's in there - could you tell her we're out of tonic...

Yeah, sure... what does she look like?

Um...um...I'm afraid you've got me there... It's not the sort of thing a chap notices after forty years...

ANSWERS

p.24 HIT. . . OR MISSED!

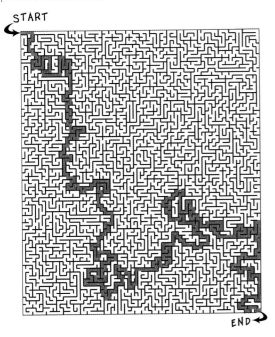

START

END

p.26 THE SHOOTING PARTY

p.36 MIX AND MATCH FOOD AND WINE QUIZ

Asparagus	Sauvignon Blanc
Christmas Pudding	Liqueur Muscat
Consommé	Fino Sherry
Foie Gras	Sauternes
Fruits de Mers	Muscadet
Goat's Cheese	Sancerre
Oysters	Champagne
Parma Ham and Melon	Pinot Grigio
Roast Lamb	Red Bordeaux
Roast Pork	Beaujolais
Roquefort	Sauternes
Stilton	Port
Strawberries and Cream	Sweet Vouvray
Sushi	German Riesling Kabinett

p.37 WINE MULTIPLE CHOICE QUIZ

Q1. *What is the normal alcohol percentage for sherry?*
Sherry normally has an alcoholic strength of between 15–20% ABV. Spirit is added to the wine thus increasing the alcohol percentage above that of a normal table wine.

Q2. *Which of the following is not a South African wine producing region?*
Mendocino county is a series of valleys created by the Russian River located in California.

Q3. *In which country is the River Spey?*
The heartland of whisky country is Speyside, named after the river, in the Highlands of Scotland. Whiskies from here tend to be fruitier and more mellow than whiskies from Island distilleries.

Q4. *Where is the wine growing region Stellenbosch?*
South Africa. Stellenbosch in South Africa has a reputation for producing some of the country's finest red wines.

Q5. *From which country does the Allegrini brand originate?*
Italy. The Allegrini family has been making wine in Valpolicella for several generations.

Q6. *What is the recommended serving temperature for Champagne?*
Chilling does mask flavour so, the finer the wine the less it will need chilling. Remember, ice with water in an ice bucket chills better than just ice.

Q7. *Neusiederlersee (a region that produces dessert wines) is in which country?*
Neusiederlersee is located in Austria.

Q8. *Which of the following was the best vintage for Chablis?*
The best vintage for Chablis from these four years was 1996.

Q9. *Penfolds Grange is made from?*
Penfolds Grange is produced from Shiraz and small quantities of Cabernet Sauvignon. The wine is capable of ageing for up to thirty years.

Q10. *In which region in France is Muscat Beaumes de Venise made?*
It is a dessert wine made in the Rhône valley.

Q11. *Which is the only firm to ferment and mature all its Champagne in small oak casks?*
Krug is the only firm still producing all its Champagne in small oak casks, an essential element for developing Krug's intense bouquet and complex flavours.

Q12. *In 1985 which illustrious St. Emilion property was stripped of its 1er Grand Cru Classé status?*
Château Beausèjour-Bécot was stripped of its 1er Grand Cru Classé status – and reinstated in 1996. It is now one of the leading 1er Grand Cru Classé 'B' properties.

Q13. *Which of the following red wines should be chilled?*
Beaujolais is best enjoyed chilled.

Q14. *What is known as a Marie-Jeanne?*
A Marie-Jeanne is 2.25 litre bottle only found in the Bordeaux region

Q15. *Who introduced vines to England?*
The Romans introduced the vine to this country.

Q16. *What do crystals in the bottom of a bottle indicate?*
Crystals are naturally occurring and come from the tartaric acid in the wine.

Q17. *The white grape Furmint blended with Harslevelu, and sometimes Muscat, produces which famous sweet wine?*
In Hungary this combination of grapes produces the famous Tokaji Aszu.

Q18. *Cloudy Bay Sauvignon Blanc is from which country?*
Cloudy Bay is the wine that helped put New Zealand on the map for making world class Sauvignon Blanc.

Q19. *The Pinot Noir grape is the dominant force in producing the red wines of Bordeaux?*
False. Pinot Noir is the dominant grape for the red wines of Burgundy.

Q20. *In which French wine region is Minervois made?*
The appellation takes its name from the Languedoc village of Minverve. Minervois is usually red, with a small amount of rosé and white produced.

Give yourself one point for every correct answer and then tot up your score. See page 39 for Dicky's verdict on your vinous know-how.

p.42 TOTTERING LEADERGRAM

1 T	2 H	3 E	4 F	5 I	6 R	7 S	8 T	9 F	10 A	11 L	12 L	13 A	14 C	15 Y	16 A	17 G	18 U	19 E	20 S	21 T	22 M	23 U	24 S	25 T
26 E	27 R	28 A	29 D	30 I	31 C	32 A	33 T	34 E	35 F	36 R	37 O	38 M	39 H	40 I	41 S	42 M	43 I	44 N	45 D	46 I	47 S	48 T	49 H	50 A
51 T	52 H	53 E	54 I	55 S	56 I	57 N	58 S	59 O	60 M	61 E	62 W	63 A	64 Y	65 B	66 E	67 H	68 O	69 L	70 D	71 E	72 N	73 S	74 U	75 C
76 H	77 P	78 H	79 R	80 A	81 S	82 E	83 S	84 A	85 S	86 H	87 O	88 W	89 S	90 W	91 E	92 E	93 T	94 O	95 F	96 Y	97 O	98 U	99 T	100 O
101 H	102 A	103 V	104 E	105 M	106 E	107 M	108 U	109 S	110 T	111 N	112 E	113 V	114 E	115 R	116 F	117 A	118 L	119 L	120 F	121 R	122 O	123 M	124 H	125 I
126 S	127 L	128 I	129 P	130 S	131 O	132 N	133 T	134 H	135 E	136 O	137 T	138 H	139 E	140 R	141 H	142 A	143 N	144 D	145 I	146 F	147 H	148 I	149 S	150 H
151 O	152 S	153 T	154 E	155 S	156 S	157 S	158 H	159 O	160 U	161 L	162 D	163 S	164 A	165 Y	166 T	167 O	168 H	169 I	170 M	171 W	172 E	173 A	174 R	175 E
176 S	177 O	178 T	179 H	180 R	181 I	182 L	183 L	184 E	185 D	186 Y	187 O	188 U	189 C	190 O	191 U	192 L	193 D	194 C	195 O	196 M	197 E	198 H	199 E	200 S
201 H	202 O	203 U	204 L	205 D	206 T	207 A	208 K	209 E	210 A	211 L	212 L	213 S	214 T	215 E	216 P	217 S	218 P	219 O	220 S	221 S	222 I	223 B	224 L	225 E
226 T	227 O	228 E	229 N	230 C	231 O	232 U	233 R	234 A	235 G	236 E	237 S	238 U	239 C	240 H	241 A	242 N	243 A	244 T	245 T	246 I	247 T	248 U	249 D	250 E

'The first fallacy a guest must eradicate from his mind is that he is, in some way, beholden. Such phrases as 'how sweet of you to have me' must never fall from his lips. On the other hand, if his hostess should say to him, 'We are so thrilled you could come', he should take all steps possible to encourage such an attitude.'

p.50 SUDOKU WITH A TWIST

Daffy's Puzzle

1								
6	4	1		9	2	3	7	
8	7	3	1	5			9	6
5			7		3	8		4
	2	5			7	6		9
	7		9	4	8			3
	3		9	6			1	4
2		8	4		6			1
9				3	1	7	6	8
	6	7	5	8		4	3	2

Dicky's Puzzle

	4	6	9	7		5	1	
	3		8	5	4		9	
7	5	9		6	3	8	2	4
6	2						5	7
9	1	5		4		3	8	2
3	7						4	9
5	6	3	4	8		2	7	1
	9		5	3	1		6	
	8	1		2	7	9	3	

p.66 SPOT THE DIFFERENCE

p.70 TOTTERING CROSSWORD

¹D	I	C	K	Y		²F	O	R	E	B	E	⁶A	R	⁷S
O		U				A		I		Y		R		I
⁸T	O	T	T	E	R	I	N	G		¹⁰G	R	I	L	L
T				A		R		H		E		S		K
Y		¹¹M	E	R	I	T		T	E	N	E	T		
M		R		L		R		T		¹³O				
¹⁴A	P	S	E		D	I	A	¹⁵B	O	L	I	C	A	L
N		S		P		A		A		Y		R		D
¹⁶G	O	H	E	A	D	L	O	N	G		¹⁹H	A	L	L
E		E		R				K		²⁰P		T		O
		²¹G	R	A	N	T		²³N	E	E	D	S		Y
²⁴T		T		P		O		O		E				A
²⁵O	L	I	V	E		²⁶W	A	T	E	R	F	O	W	L
U		L				E		E		F				T
²⁸T	R	E	A	S	U	R	E	S		²⁹D	A	F	F	Y

p.88 TOTTERING WORD CHAIN

Daffy, Daffs, Duffs, Tuffs, Tufts, Tifts, Lifts, Lists, Lusts, Dusts, Ducts, Ducks, Ducky, Dicky